This Pilgrim's Progress coloring book belongs to:

☐ ☐ ☐ ☐ ☐ ☐ ☐ ☐ ☐ ☐ ☐ ☐ ☐ ☐ ☐

Copyright 2019 Arianna Francis Art

www.ariannafrancisart.com

John Bunyan

John Bunyan Dreaming

John Bunyan Preaching

Christian leaves The City of Destruction

The Slough of Despond

Goodwill shows Christian the way

Goodwill shows Christian the way

In view of the cross

Christian meets Mistrust & Timorous

Christian meets Mistrust and Timorous

Watchful

Notwithstanding the Lord stood with me, and strengthened me; that by me the preaching might be fully known, and that all the Gentiles might hear: and I was delivered out of the mouth of the lion. And the Lord shall deliver me from every evil work, and will preserve me unto his heavenly kingdom: to whom be glory for ever and ever. Amen.

-2 Timothy 4:17-18

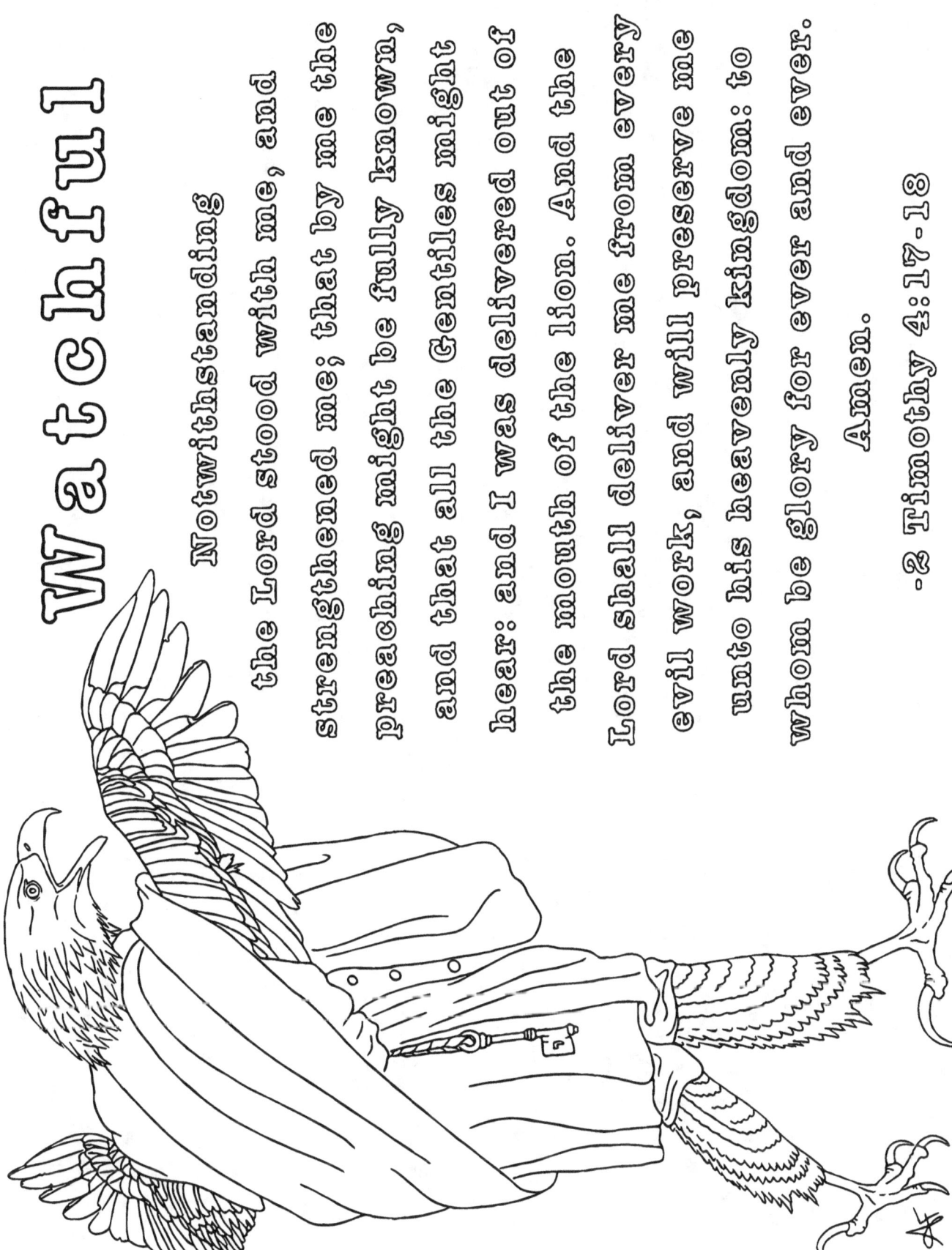

Watchful

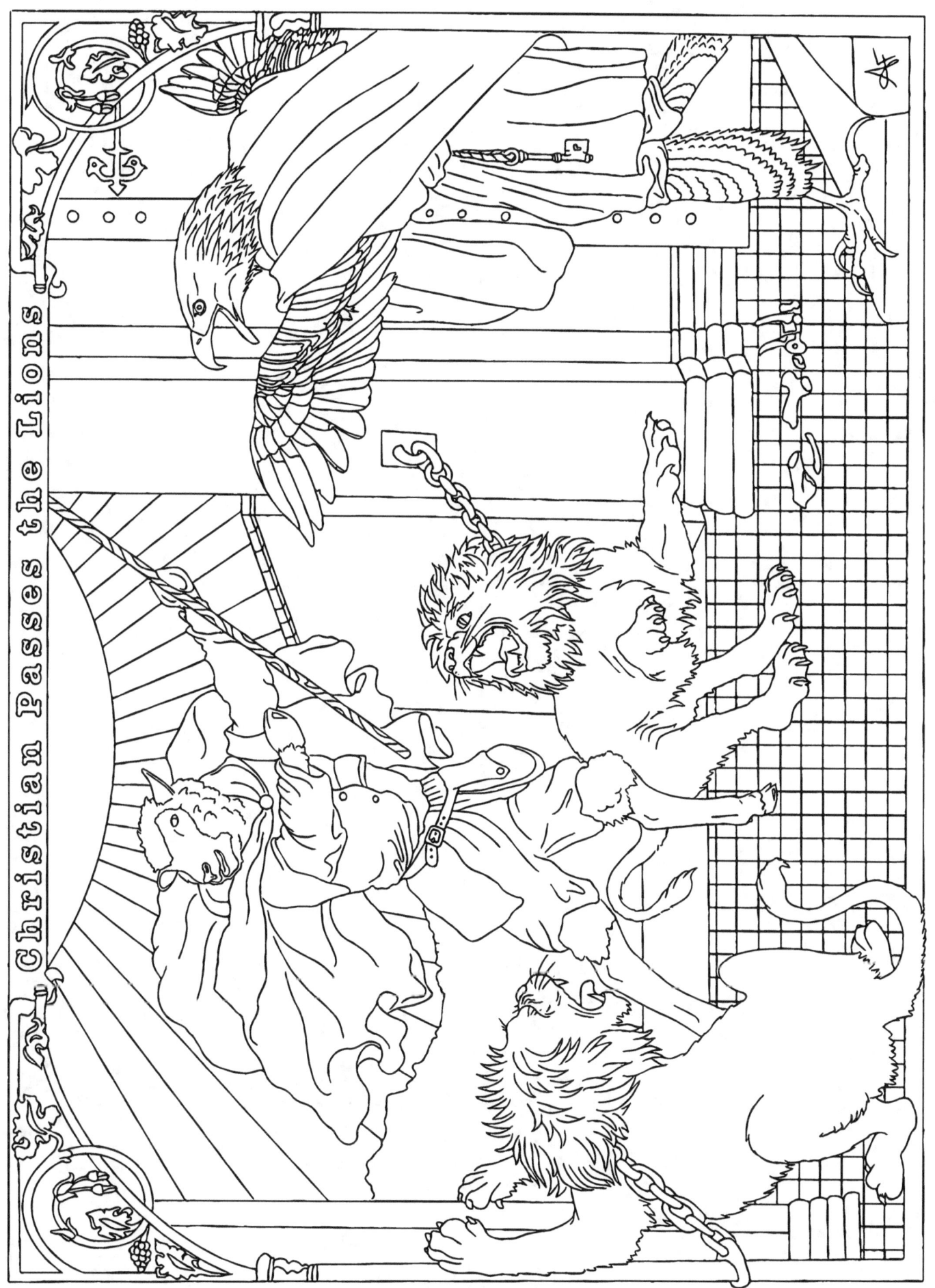

Passing the Lions

Christian armed by Prudence, Discretion, Piety & Charity

Christian at the Palace

Giant Pope threatens Christian

Giant Pope

Faithful's Struggle

Evangelist Councils

Death at Vanity Fair

Mr. By-ends

He that walketh righteously, and speaketh uprightly; he that despiseth the gain of oppressions, that shaketh his hands from holding of bribes, that stoppeth his ears from hearing of blood, and shutteth his eyes from seeing evil; He shall dwell on high: his place of defence shall be the munitions of rocks: bread shall be given him; his waters shall be sure. Thine eyes shall see the king in his beauty: they shall behold the land that is very far off.
-Isaiah 33:15-17

Mr. By-ends

Mr. Money-love's lesson in hypocrisy

Mr. Money-love

Talkative

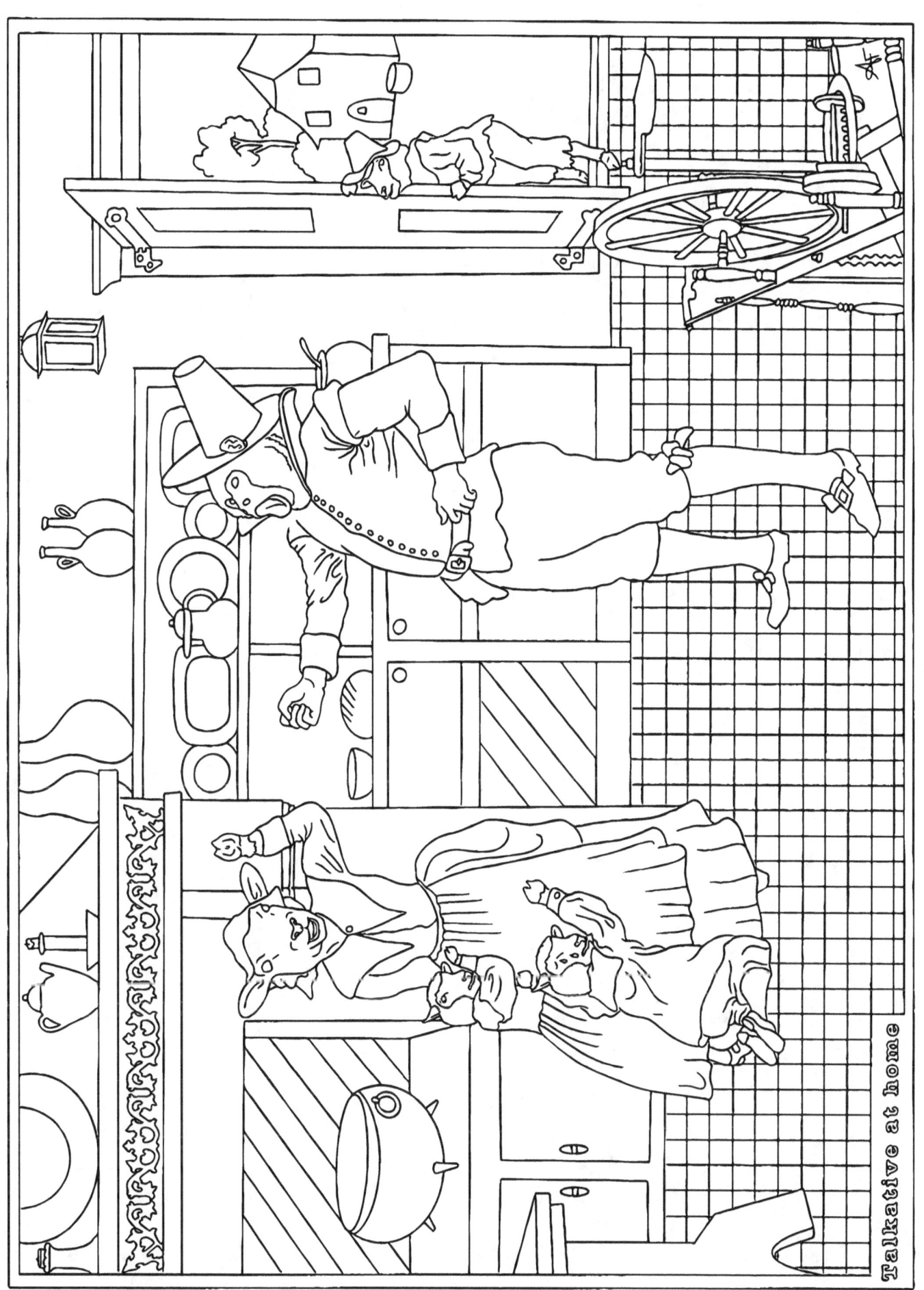

Talkative at home

Talkative at home

Castle of Giant Despair

Little-faith robbed

Enchanted Ground

Christian instructs Ignorance

Hopeful advises Temporary

Entering the Celestial City

www.ingramcontent.com/pod-product-compliance
Lightning Source LLC
Chambersburg PA
CBHW081700220526

45466CB00009B/2827